DEDICATION

For my granddad, who told me that this was an excellent idea and for those who have kept me growing as a writer and as a person.

CONTENTS

ACKNOWLEDGMENTS

Thanks to all those who've heard me complain about this endeavor for who knows how long. I also appreciate my gin and Morrissey records. They really pulled through for me.

Lost

Writing

Inspiration has struck me once or twice, but I have not yet been killed.

A World's Stage

Blank stare.
Sweeping thoughts.
     Buzzing about in romantic fashion.
Outside of element,
Desiring reality,
Cameras flashing.

Bearing the scars and stories of fiction,
What we desire as creatures of the theatre
When the great actors of life have portrayed us with ill
intent.

God, separate us from our mortal intentions.

Goodbye, Wonderful World.
     Hello to purity of heart.
          We have bitten from the apple,
          Facing demons of our own.

My own deluded stage picture,
The audience of humanity
     Is stunned
     In starving silence.

Burden

I am three years old.
I am on my mother's hip.
Her name was Tracy. She was twelve.
Her name was Danieal. She was four.

They had Cerebral Palsy.
Their abusers framed as saints.
They are dead.

I am nine years old.
I am forgetting my name, but remembering theirs.
I am not on my mother's hip.
I am not in my mother's arms.
I am not her daughter.
I am Cerebral Palsy.
My mother is a saint.
She has forgotten my name.

My friend, confined in the same way that I am, announces joyously that sometimes, she wants to kill herself so that she can dance with Jesus, sooner rather than later. For a moment, I agree, because I have forgotten my name, too.

It isn't long, however, before I learn to answer to the word "burden."

I am "Burden."

I am sixteen years old.
It is my birthday.
I am eating Key Lime Pie.
The Saint made it for me because it is my favorite.
She then turns to me and asks, "Do you ever wish you'd

died?"
The question resounds around the quiet kitchen and I
wonder if she knows that I have counted the number of
sleeping pills we have again.

I am eighteen.
The Saint tells me, "Get the fuck out of my house."
I wonder if she noticed that my bags have been packed for
years.
It is Christmas.
She visits.
Calls me by name.
"Burden."
I slam the door.

I am twenty-one.
A gentleman tells me that he knows my name.
It isn't long before I believe him.
He then decides that it tastes bitter in his mouth.
Spits out "Woman" instead.
I no longer answer.

I am twenty-four.
I have Cerebral Palsy.
I am Adina.
Her name was Tracy.
Her name was Danieal.

Our abusers walk free as saints.
Our secrets are confided in the graves of two little girls
And the set of caged birds that rise and fall
With pleading in my voice.

Remember us.
Please remember us.

Hope is Full

She opened the door and stepped outside to the world
unknown
       Without setting foot on the ground.

I tried to capture her the way one tries to capture fireflies
in glass houses,
       With too much faith, and too little grace.

Gardening Indifference

You told me that my neck tasted of Honeysuckle
Whenever you offered kisses.

Covering the bruises that you and I both called
"Caught in the moment accidents."

You called me your Rose,
Covered with thorns to wound,

But delicate.

I don't like Roses.
Come to think of it,
I don't care for Honeysuckles either.

Too bad I don't have the heart to tell you.

Two

I try and cover you up
With things from my dreams, like a blanket of warm snow.
I try to hide you in curves.

Two.
The cages of two.
I wonder often if you remember the winter snow and how
untouched it looked in my backyard,
Until you stumbled into me with your bloodied jacket.
I'm trying to describe you, but I can't.
I can't.
You were something of a satanic safe haven for me.

Two.
The souls of two.
I wonder if you remember the conversations on faith, on
love –

Hush, hush, there's no such thing.
Strumming on your strings,
You sang to my body more than anything.
I was something you could fit in your travelin' pocket.
In the spring, when life started over,
You and I would scan the horizons for nothing in
particular.

Are you a dreamer still?

Do you lie awake?
Are you one to sleep on the world?
I miss you, friend.

For now, here's two cents you can fit
In your travelin' pocket.

Goodnight –
I hope the stars are out,
So you don't lose your way

Again.

Evolving

Here is a poem to tell of change and paint you a picture,
Without colorful words or imagery.

Change will come in evolution;
Evolution will come when my hands sprout wings,

And my confined, **black** and white words
Can free themselves of pages.

Remember Me, One?

Remember me?
>Do you?

Remember the noises that unsettled in the night,
With the whispers and the taunting of past lovers as you
tried to hold me tight?
How about the waves that I cast upon your shore,
expecting you to be a tide ever-returning.
I cannot hold anything against you, not of my sins nor my
convictions,
Let alone let you touch me, even if it is burning –
>This yearning

To feel you, to taste you;
>To make a beautiful mess of you;
>To waste;
>To toss you up with words you'd never believe;
The children and the dreams we'd never conceive.
I want to feel you moving beneath my veins
>Yet you remain still,
>The rock;
And I, the battering sands of time.
Never again will you hold these hands of mine.

Death of a Child

Tug on the hem of my skirt.

Watering.

Nothing is there.

Warnings

I should have known by that "Beware of the Dog" sign at
our church entrance that you were dangerous.
By "church" I mean our shitty home.
Shitty because you promised to worship me,
And I instead bowed at your feet.
By "Beware of the Dog" sign, I mean the cackles
And the shit-eating grin you flashed
Each time you called me "bitch."
It was you who bared your teeth, not I.

I told others about you as though you carved out stars in
the sky.
You were the one who fed and clothed me,
For I was wicked.

Naked. Alone.

I sang about you as though you had given me reason,
But you were the one who stole my voice.

And when you beat me with open fists,
I wanted to blame the stigmata.

words that weigh a lot:

sorry
afraid
careful
call
no
yes
maybe
leaving
left
go
stop
please
forgot
miss
have
want
need
thanks
empty
you
me
myself
I
am
it
space
starting
new
begin
remember
home

Rude Houseguest

My feverish memories and quiet demons are all too quick
to become my friends,

Despite not being much for conversation.

Bare Walls

If walls could talk, I'm certain mine would rather scream at
the collection of empty liquor bottles,
And the letters that you wrote me with equally empty
intention.

The words you wrote meant nothing,
A shroud in rose-colored glasses,
And nothing but the quiet embrace of paper,
As these walls screech in agony on my behalf.

Chaos

Coming and going,
In waves of staying in bed,
In waves of silence,
In the still of madness.

Before hitting the shores,

I crash and drown.

Viewpoint

Curtains can only cover so much,
> Just as birds can only sing tunes so many times,
> Letting the wind carry their wings.

As I yearn for a bird's eye view,
> I can only let the past go so many times
> Before it comes back,

> Like the bellowing sea finds friendship in the shore.

Chubby Bunny

When I first tell you I love you
The words will fall out onto the floor
And I will attempt to shove them back far within myself
As though I'm determined to win
The most intense game of chubby bunny ever
And then they'll still spill out.

The words *I love you* are not meaningless.
They will float around
Like the majority of fluttered birds
When we first free them from their cages
Much like my lungs
Or the weight within my chest right now
When I first tell you I love you.

I assure you that this had gone far better in the shower
And there was some crying.
It was an Oscar-winning performance, I swear to god.
I'm sorry I'm a mess right now
But when I first tell you I love you, it's theatrical
I think I'm putting on a farce.
I hope it's a good farce.
I hope it's a good sex farce at least.

Maybe, possibly, I don't know how this goes.
I don't know how this works.
Hell, my legs don't even work
So pardon my stumbling.
I'm a very tiny woman
But these words take up space
And I know because my voice
Takes up space as well.

When I enter a space, I announce myself and you know it.

A BIRD'S EYE

You noticed without me speaking,
Uttering a word.
You know it.
You noticed far more than this.
Perhaps you noticed my hair
Or my eyes
Or the curl of my smirk.

I don't know a goddamn thing
But I know one thing.
I love you,
And that's all I want to say.

But this is far beyond
Some intense game of chubby bunny.

Pardon me, I choked on a couple of marshmallows there.
Chubby Bunny Chubby Bubby Chubby Bunny.
I love you I love you I love you.
I'm sorry I'm a mess.
I love you.

Selective

Forgetting is an art form that my heart has yet to master,
Because I still hear the curve of your body echo in my
    sheets.
I've become used to your presence in the ceiling fan,
Tasting your lips in the syrup on my pancakes
And feeling your hand in the hollow of my palm.

Fanned

"Anything," she said, "is better than this."

I could present you as something stoic, because at least
then
 – My statue, Marble –

I'd have an explanation as to why you are so cold.

But even marble can be shifted,
With determination and weathering winds.
However, that takes time and permanency.
The way you left my side so abruptly leads me to believe,
that you
 – My sculptor –

Have neither of those things.

Bibles

Her bones call to me in the way that crows are beckoned
to forlorn churchyards –

Slowly,
Overwhelmingly,
Consuming.

no title

Love.

It's not timeless, but it simply loses track.
The nights are quiet and still, and it's okay.
You like it that way.

It lights up the sidewalks, and dark alleys are guided.
It doesn't matter if one wanders off,
As you'll find another who lights up your path

Again.

Skip off into summer and I use your eyes;

A pillow for my defeat of tired mornings and slumber less
nights.
You, safe haven for my blanket of woes lying beneath my
lids,
Heavy and thick
As your breath in the evening air.

Sitting down on my bed,
I lose track.
We lose track,
Growing old after all.

While in a Car

Remember getting caught eating alone in the high school
bathroom stall?
Remember how her lips tasted like fruit loops,
So you ate nothing
But a box of those fucking things for weeks?
What the fuck was that about?

Why did I have to taste our heartbreak more than once?

Does he know his hand is on my thigh?
Is this a thing?

I think it's a thing.

. . . How do I tell you how poor your taste in music is?
Hey, at least you didn't have to go through that weird
horse phase in fifth grade.

He's holding my hand.
Holy shit.
He's holding my hand and I wonder if I'll ever stop the
quivering anticipation that lies
Within the fear of him raising *his told me later*.

Please turn this song up.
It's Born to Run, for crying out loud.

REMEMBER THAT REALLY EMBARRASSING
THING THAT HAPPENED IN THIRD GRADE?

THE ONE YOU DESPERATELY TRY
AND BLOCK OUT.

That's the one.

That last remaining cigarette on your dashboard looks just
as lonely as we are
together.
It's a good thing I'm sitting down most of the time so he
doesn't know
exactly how weak
he makes me in the knees.

Are we lost?

. . . Am I lost?

Do you know how to take a left turn?
Jesus Christ.
We're here.
Fucking finally.
We're here.
I'm here. I'm here.
I think I'm here.

Page Summary

Love

I want so desperately to end this chapter,

But I

Cannot bring myself to

Turn the page.

Untouchable

When my Sarah told me she was one of the gods, I
    brought myself to my knees,
Not to beg for forgiveness, but for some scrap of
    innocence.

Like drowning in the bathtub as one attempts to scrub
    away their mortal flaws,
I carried the weight of her guilt in Samson's hair and
    awoke myself to caring.

Purest December

You always loved me in the month of December,
Claiming you hated the snow because of the cool air.
But I know the truth:
You were trapped with me.
Like a moth to a flame, you longed for something you
could no longer touch.
Funny thing, though;

You never liked change.
                    The holidays sickened you.
                                        Me too.

I was always lonely by then,
Much more so than before;
Insisting that you never needed to buy me gifts,
Because all I wanted was something that could never be
purchased –
Unless I wanted to be your toy and have you call me baby
For a few hours . . .
But even then.

You sang along with Christmas carols because, "That's the
way you were raised."
Then, you lit the candles with me,
Always making a point to splatter hot chocolate on the
carpet.
I think you just wanted an excuse to see me on my hands
and knees,
Cleaning up after you.
I told you it was okay
Because nothing in love is clean.

Not even the whitest snow.

Empty

If I could grant you a few wishes

In silence,
In being LOUD,
In being small and quiet,
In being nothing at all,

I would.

But to wish is to pine after what one cannot afford,
And I have no pennies to toss into the well.

Instrumental

I sliced you open, and pulled you back – screaming in
      piano keys and moaning in the requiem into sweet
      hours of morning birds.
Trying to master the tunes of your body like the tone of
      the organ once played in church.

Bent out of shape you were, rusted and cold with your
      curled toes,
Hitting the right notes only once
Before we finished the masterpiece and succumbed to
      restless nights.

Awake you'd be, with the ring on your finger playing to
      guilt,
                But only after the act was over.

Strumming him along with fiddles of forgotten beings,
Singing like a raven, with forlorn song.

              If only to yourself;
          A symphony for a sinful act.

Wet Socks

I find that my loneliness is seeping onto the soles of
passers-by.

I wonder if they notice,

Or if I'm just to be stomped on in the rain.

Entryway

I thought it was in the leftover cookies
Or in the art of mine you kept on the fridge.
In the stomping of little feet down the hall,
In his arms after the war.
Or in her eyes as she sang me to sleep,
On couches and pullout beds,
Hotel rooms,
Floors.

But perhaps home is nowhere.
Home is no place at all.
Within myself,
A haven and several secrets – mine to keep.
And no "Welcome Home" lantern burns brighter
Than that of a peaceful soul beckoning sleep.

A Glimmer

Turn down the lights
Brightly burning their worn eyes,
A love that's tested time
As her memory fades,

Like the gray that crowns her head.

Remember . . .

Remember . . .

A look of concern,
Confusion over candlelit dinners,
The woman he has known has faded,
And his heart along with her.
Diving into the fountain of youth,
Treasured heart in the palm of one's hand
Dragged off to the bottom of the seas.

But the fountain of youth carries no memory.
He dives in after her ghostly silhouette,
Capturing the heart
That she treasured,
Both bodies consumed in the waters of memories.

So, if you hear of the two
Widows whispering,
Sparrows singing against the swallowed-word shore,
Recollect your memories,
As you wait for time to fade.

They become so much more,
As the fountain of youth is but lust.
Such gold is far more prized in the present time.

Kinship

And who am I to question you
      At times on roads ahead?

By and by I go again
      To the mortal way

Aching once to touch;
      Begging twice to feel,
            In highest hopes you'll stay

Hamlet's Foolery

Care to explain so much again?
The way in which you dance, move and sway speaks
nothing of my affections for you.
In fact, it foreshadows Doomsday.
Perhaps we quarrel, and then we shall wed,
Nothing but hatred and lust lying in bed.
Oh! 'Tis but a state of mind, they say
But never shall they feel this way.
Lust takes one glance;
Love a journey.
Lies take upon the wings of one's fragile mind.

Ghosts

Ghosts –
Of history, of past, of present –
Show vulnerability.
I shiver;

> You put your fingers upon me,
> And slowly your hand paints curves;
> A shape I know is of a different young woman.

> "Oh my god, darling . . .
> You're like a porcelain doll."
> I know.

Childhood things can be put away and allowed to fade
    fondly,
> But here I am,
> Exposed to you.

> "It's okay."

> You try and accept it.
> The scars on my ever-skinny legs,
> Tired of never walking down the aisle;
> Of never walking down the street.

> My feet swollen,
> And you're studying everything like a carpenter.
> You wince.
> I'm crying now.

I know it's all in my head, just as you are with me – distant.
As you once again think about her while touching me,
The imperfect ghost
Of failure.

"What did this to you?"
"Who did this to you?"

My ivory skin just peels itself back, as I look at you in
silence,
Hazel eyes blank.
"The ghosts of life."
The ghosts of decisions that weren't made soon enough.
The ghosts of your discontentment with my body,
With me.

"Does this hurt?"
"Don't worry."

You won't break me,
But then again,
You won't love me either.
You stand up straight, as though nothing happened.
I crookedly offer you a hand again.
You kiss my neck out of hunger for someone, something
else.

Like taking a bite from a rotten apple,
But I take it.
Because everyone has ghosts,
And although you don't see yours,
I do.

Every. Single. Damn. Time.
And never dared to walk with me.

I am your ghost, yet . . .
You're the one haunting me.
You. Lay. Your. Lively. Hands. Upon. Me.

Wall Art

I try and describe your shapes in the way I approach the
canvas.

With different hues and purposeful intentions,
Unknown to you, of course.

My affections for you could never be mounted on a wall
anyway.

Puzzle

I know two things about love:
      You lose your heart;
Then,
      You lose your . . . I forgot.

                 It's not all about numbers, letters;

One simple train of thought.
If love was as simplistic as we tend to make it
      in movies,
As tragic as it seems to be
      in books . . .

If writers wrote the way one speaks about love –
      Or, if the study of logic was dead
                 (Which it is,
                 Because the loss of love
            Has no logic, and knows no bounds),

And mathematics will tell you the probability –
      not of one

         f
       a
      l
        l
          i
            n
              g

                Nothing.
                I forgot.
                I know nothing.

Passive

When you've grown tired of brokenness, let me know,
And allow me to count the ways,
With pill bottles and sleeping for days.
I'm not sure if the hollows of your cheeks can hold my
hopes anymore.

Your needle marks might.

Monster

I became a feminist when I woke up and realized that the
women in my family were taught to shrink.
I told myself to take up space.

I became a feminist when you called your mother a cunt
with angered eyes and quivering lip.
Boys don't cry, but they threaten to drag you by your hair.

I became a feminist when you told me that "rape" was just
another word for violation,
As you proceeded to violate me for several months.

I became a feminist when you announced my gender
rather than lovingly calling my name.
I became a feminist when you pinned me down and told
me to shut up.

I rose,

Clawing, screaming and reclaiming my name.

You created your own monster.

I became a feminist after returning home from your war.

Just

The heart beats at an average of 60–100 beats per minute.
Though her hope is faint, her pulse is not.
You can close the bedroom door now.
You can stop watching her sleep now.

Those lines around her lips were not brought on by
laughter and joy over the years, but rather the cigarettes
she's hung around her lips and a mouth that refuses to
speak.

You will find where the investment lies in your medicine
cabinet.
Although it won't be much;
A few glazed-over eyes and silent dinners are better
Than suicide threats and wet shoulders.

You are a child.
You are not a Necromancer.
You are a child.
No amount of "I love you, Mom"
No amount of "I met this boy today, Mom"
No amount of "I wrote this for you, Mom"
Will ever bring her back.
Even if you were a Necromancer,
You cannot wake the willing dead.

Close the door.
The heart beats at an average of 60–100 beats per minute.

See?

She's just sleeping.

Atoms

I had surrendered to you all that I thought I was.

She was nothing.

You were nothing –

A cold corpse,
A forgotten man,
Living in the shell of a boy.

Tell me, do you live still?
Or are you waiting for your nothings
To become somethings?

I Want

Coffee and Dean Martin records;
The scent of you to linger in my clothes and trickle down
    my throat;
Casual conversation in anything but casualwear;
       To be painted on,
       Torn down,
       Ripped apart;
           Lace gowns,
           Silly silhouettes;
To count the wounds that infest your hands:
       One;
           Two;
               Three;
                   Four.

In the morning,
I'll call you back later.
Your t-shirt is in my closet.
It doesn't smell of you anymore.

Like the Sun

You'Ve arrivEd.

It's amazing how a little lighting changes everything,

Shining so brightly within the cool, dark ruins of one's own corrupt mind,

SteaLing the shOw.

Over Again

Just quiet down.
Just quiet down and restart now.
Just forget the beginning and go to the end.

Where you and I are bound to destroy again.
A rhythm of paper,
A rhyme of reason,
I don't have the time for any of that.

Darling, if love is a concept,
Then you are a law that defies science.

Writhing hands and feeble bones,
Brilliant minds and glowing souls
Light my skyline.
Take me home.
Let us end again.

Sacrifice

"I admire your faith," she said, as she led me to the
    gallows.
"How can I not believe?" I grinned, "With such a beautiful
    testament to this earth?"

The air was untouched.
My father had left me with a blank canvas to paint, and
    sole-less shoes to fill.
She, my Mary, was soft and delicate as a resurrected
    sparrow.

The taunts were overwhelming, but I took them, just as I
    took all of her.
Her eyes of lust glancing about with entrancing thought,
Her ivory skin of gluttony,
Which settled in so perfectly with the tailored suits and
    carats of diamond drapery,
Her hands of envy, which longed to have my power in
    their grasp;
Her feet of fury – quick, and calloused;
Her hair of sloth, knotted in neglect and combed with
    carelessness.

But her heart of pride,
So misguided, chose to guide me here.
With upturned face and a downwards soul,
"Forgive me love, for I know not what I do.
I know I tempt,
I know I stray,
But this.
Listen,
Listen please.
I need you.
Hear what I say.

"I only stray when you wish to keep me,
I only tempt when others turn their head.
To the gallows we shall go together."

She took my hand,
Sin and sacrifice shall never wake the dead.
The dead – you say – are sleeping,
And in dreams they lie awake,
Within their coffins ringing bells,
Restlessness,
Our peace they take.
You took my peace,
You've been haunting me,
Blaming me for sleep.

Now, it's my guilt you keep.
Carry your cross;
It's yours to bear
I did not lead you to the gallows –
Your actions led you there.

Incomplete

I felt you slip through my fingers before we started loving,
       Igniting a match at both ends.
You constantly left your laughter in the kitchen sink
Among my mess of dishes and nothing was done.
       Nothing will ever be done.

Mister Rogers

I wanted to tell you what I learned today,
As you sat there
With your newspaper
And tired coffee cup.

You loved from a distance.
Talking about the magic of planes, trains, and automobiles.

As Mister Rogers told me, "It's you, I like."

I asked you about that once,
About how sometimes you could,
And sometimes you couldn't.

I wonder if Mister Rogers knows about "sometimes."

Or if he must always don the "I like you" replies like his
sweaters.
I wish you would wear my "I like you" –
It'd look rather handsome on you.

Guidance

The city never sleeps alone
For I am among the highways in restlessness,
The darkened night,
The bus lines.
Counting all the steps you took
To finally walk away.

Key

"Be open,"
You ordered.

As you closed the gates to what I thought we had,
I pried them back open,
Picking the locks of cruelty and making a skeleton key of
    honesty,

Unleashing all the skeletons in my closet,
Hoping we could join them
In the death of new beginnings.

Take Me, April

Take me to August,
Where the roads are painted green,
And the hurt was mended in what your mother seamed.

June was where I fell
Deeper and deeper,
Into this "love" we call hell.

Paint me a July, steadfast and true.
Nothing is broken, except maybe you.

Walk me through September,
Of autumns painted black;
Innocence tainted,
Ghosts calling back.

Recall a November of deafening wind,
A December of goose-pimples and skin paper-thin.
Call me in March, when wisdom is due;
April, my April, please always be true.

My calendar's not numbered.
Months fly by without a wink of sleep,
I'm envious of a secret I can no longer keep.
The years hold long,
The Spirit's breaking;
Which is why for you, I'm begging.

Take me back to August,
Where roads were painted green,

And happiness
Was just as simple as it seemed,
With no more disruptions
From child-like dreams.

49964141R10042

Made in the USA
Lexington, KY
26 February 2016